REDUCE, REUSE, RECYCLE!

Clothes and Toys

Deborah Chancellor

PowerKiDS
press.

New York

Published in 2010 by The Rosen Publishing Group Inc.
29 East 21st Street, New York, NY 10010

Copyright © 2010 Wayland/The Rosen
Publishing Group, Inc.

First Edition

Editor: Katie Powell
Designer: Elaine Wilkinson
Consultant: Kate Ruttle
Picture Researcher: Shelley Noronha
Photographer: Andy Crawford

Library of Congress Cataloging-in-Publication Data

Chancellor, Deborah.
  Clothes and toys / Deborah Chancellor. -- 1st ed.
    p. cm. -- (Reduce, reuse, recycle)
  Includes index.
  ISBN 978-1-61532-232-9 (library binding)
  ISBN 978-1-61532-238-1 (paperback)
  ISBN 978-1-61532-239-8 (6-pack)
  1. Recycling industry. 2. Clothing and dress. 3. Toys. I. Title.
  HD9975.A2.C43 2010
  363.72'82--dc22

                    2009023772

Photographs:
Cover: © Ecoscene/Ed Maynard. pg 1 Wayland, 2 Recycle Now, 4 Patrick Bennett/CORBIS, 5 Brad Killer/Istock, 6 Sean
Locke/Istock, 7 Recycle Now, 8 Ed Maynard/ Ecoscene, 8 Recycle Now, 10 Christine Osborne/Ecoscene, 11 James L.
Amos/CORBIS,12 Istock, 13 Recycle Now, 14 Wayland, 15 moodboard/Corbis, 16 Wayland, 17 Peter Morgan/Reuters/Corbis,
18 Corbis Sygma, 19 Wayland, 20 Peter Usbeck /Alamy, 21 Uwe Krejci/zefa/Corbis, 22 Jupiterimages/Ablestock/Alamy, 23
Patrick Robert/Sygma/Corbis, 24 Getty images, 25 Istock, 26 Recycle Now, 27 Melvyn Longhurst / Alamy, 28, 29 Wayland,
Cover: Ed Maynard/Ecoscene.

With thanks to RecycleNow for kind permission to reproduce the photographs on the imprint page, 7, 9, 13, and 26.

The author and publisher would like to thank the following models: Lawrence Do of Scotts Park Primary School,

Manufactured in China
CPSIA Compliance Information: Batch #WAW0102PK: For Further Information
contact Rosen Publishing, New York, New York at 1-800-237-9932

Contents

Words in **bold** can be found in the glossary.

What a waste!

Every day, we throw away huge amounts of garbage. Most of it is taken to garbage dumps called **landfill sites**, where it is crushed and buried. A small amount of our trash is burned in big **furnaces** called **incinerators**.

◀ Garbage is collected from trash cans outside our homes in waste collection trucks.

Did You Know?

In the United States, most children get more than ten toys a year. This adds up to 600 million new toys.

We can **reduce** waste by being careful about what we throw out. A lot of toys and clothes don't need to be thrown away. If they are in a good **condition**, they can be **reused** by someone else. If this isn't possible, maybe they can be **recycled** and turned into something new.

◀ *This woman is making a new bag from some old clothes.*

5

Reduce, reuse, recycle

Clothes and toys do not last forever. People grow out of them, or they get worn out. You can reduce the amount of toys and clothes you throw away. Before you get rid of anything, think how it could be reused or recycled.

◀ *Some clothes that are bought are never worn. This is very wasteful.*

Giving toys and clothes away when they are not wanted anymore means they can be reused by someone else. If they are damaged, it may be possible to take them to a **recycling bank**. They will be collected from there and sorted at a **recycling center**.

◄ Most clothes can be recycled at a **clothing bank** like this one.

Did You Know? More than half of the world's **population** wears secondhand clothes. Think before you throw something away. Someone else may need it, somewhere else in the world.

Materials for clothes

Materials that are made from threads are called **textiles**. There are two kinds of textiles—**natural** and **man-made**. Cotton, wool, and silk are natural textiles. Man-made textiles include nylon and polyester. Nearly all textiles can be recycled.

◀ *Unwanted clothes are being sorted at this recycling center.*

You Can Help!

When you take shoes to a shoe bank, tie the laces together or put a rubber band around them, so they don't get separated.

Another natural material is leather. Leather is made from the skin of animals, such as cows. It is often used to make shoes and boots. Leather can be recycled or reused, for example, you can take your old shoes to a **shoe bank**.

Saving clothes

Reusing and recycling our old clothes saves **raw materials**, such as cotton and wool, and saves **energy**, such as **electricity**, in factories. It also cuts down on the **pollution** made by clothes factories, for example, when textiles are **dyed** and **bleached**.

◄ Cotton fibers are found in the seed pods of the cotton plant. Cotton crops are grown around the world.

Factories can also reduce clothes waste. Leftover threads can be collected and reused. Unwanted scraps of material called remnants can be sold and reused for crafts such as rug making. Scraps can also be shredded to make stuffing for mattresses and furniture.

LOOKING AFTER YOUR CLOTHES

1. Wear an apron or an old shirt if you are doing something messy.

2. Wear old clothes for playing outside.

▲ *This man is using remnants to make some furniture cushions.*

Wear it again

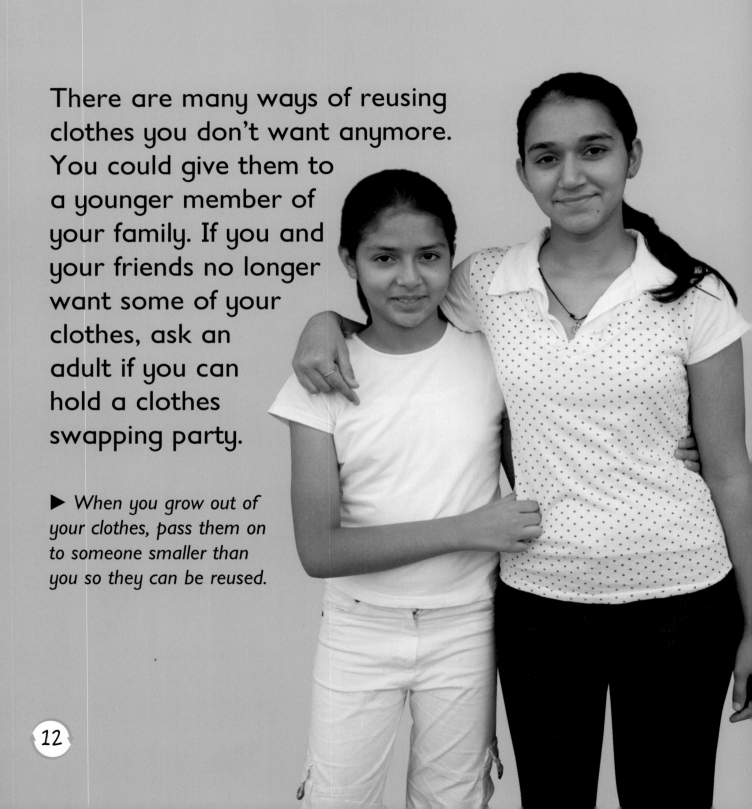

There are many ways of reusing clothes you don't want anymore. You could give them to a younger member of your family. If you and your friends no longer want some of your clothes, ask an adult if you can hold a clothes swapping party.

▶ *When you grow out of your clothes, pass them on to someone smaller than you so they can be reused.*

▶ *Whenever you can, buy clothes from charity-driven thrift stores. You are reusing clothes, and giving money to help people in need.*

You Can Help!

Before you give your clothes away to a thrift store, wash and fold them, and put them in a bag to keep them in a good condition.

Unwanted clothes can be given to a **thrift store**. Some may be sold at the store. Others will be given away to homeless people or to people who have been hurt in a **natural disaster**. They may also be given to poor people in Africa and Asia.

Recycling clothes

When we recycle our clothes, we turn waste clothes into new things. Threads are taken from old clothes and used to make new clothes, or other useful things. Woolen clothes, for example, can be sorted into different colors so the yarn may be used again.

◀ *The yarn from this knitted sweater could be* **unraveled** *to make a blanket or a scarf.*

Did You Know?

New clothes can be made from recycled plastic bottles. It takes 25 big beverage bottles to make one large fleece.

In the U.S., only a little of the space in clothing banks is used. Ask an adult to help you find your nearest clothing bank. Clothes from the bank are taken away to be sorted. Damaged clothes may be sold to factories, cut up, and made into cleaning cloths.

◀ Keep a basket at home for any clothes that cannot be reused. When it is full, take it to the clothing bank.

Too many toys

Children today have more toys than ever before. One way to reduce the amount of toys we throw away is not to buy so many of them. Next time you are shopping, think before you buy a new toy, or ask for one as a present. Do you really need it?

◀ Over half of all toys are thrown away before they are worn out or broken.

▲ *Look on the packaging. It tells you where it was made.*

There are lots of reasons to buy fewer new toys. Some toys travel a long way from the country where they were made to the place where they are sold. This uses lots of **fuel** and energy, and causes pollution, which is bad for the **environment**.

Did You Know?

Eight out of ten toys sold around the world are made in China. A doll made in China travels more than 7,000 miles to be sold in a store in New York or Chicago.

Toy materials

Toys are made from many different materials. Some are made from natural materials such as wood, and some are made from man-made materials, such as fur fabric or plastic. When plastic toys are dumped in landfill sites, they take 500 years to **decay.**

▲ *Most stuffed toys are made with fur fabric. This is a man-made material.*

Many electronic toys and games are made with materials that can be recycled. Old game consoles and games do not have to be thrown away. Stores will often buy old games from you to resell and may also be able to tell you where they can be recycled.

▲ If you throw an electronic toy away, take out the batteries first so they can be recycled.

BATTERIES

1. Don't throw batteries away in your trash can. Batteries have **chemicals** inside them that cause pollution.

2. You can take old batteries to special local recycling points.

3. Use **rechargeable** batteries for your electronic toys and games, so you don't keep buying and recycling batteries.

4. Ask an adult to plug your electronic game into a wall socket so you don't need batteries at all.

Toy packaging

Many new toys are wrapped in strong, bulky packaging. Some packaging stops toys from getting broken when they travel from the factory to the store. But a lot of it is unnecessary. Making packaging in factories also uses energy.

◄ *This store has lots of toys wrapped in packaging. Most of this packaging will end up as waste.*

When toy packaging is thrown away, it usually ends up in landfill sites. Toy packaging is made from different materials, for example, paper, cardboard, and plastic. Most of these materials can be easily recycled, but they must be separated and sorted first.

◀ *After a birthday party, sort out your toy packaging carefully. Save all the parts that can be recycled.*

Pass it on

Reusing toys may mean people buy fewer new ones. Look after your toys, so they don't break. That way, you will be able to pass them on to someone else.

▲ *Clean your toys before you give them away and ask an adult to check that they are working properly.*

You could **donate** your old toys to a charity thrift store. By giving your toys to charity, someone else in another country will be able to reuse your unwanted toys.

▲ This little girl in Africa is playing with a toy donated by charity.

CLEAR OUT YOUR CLOSET

1. You could give your toys to friends or to members of your family.

2. Ask a parent to donate some of your toys to the children's ward at your nearest hospital.

3. You could organize a toy stand at your school rummage sale to sell unwanted toys.

23

Sell, swap, or borrow

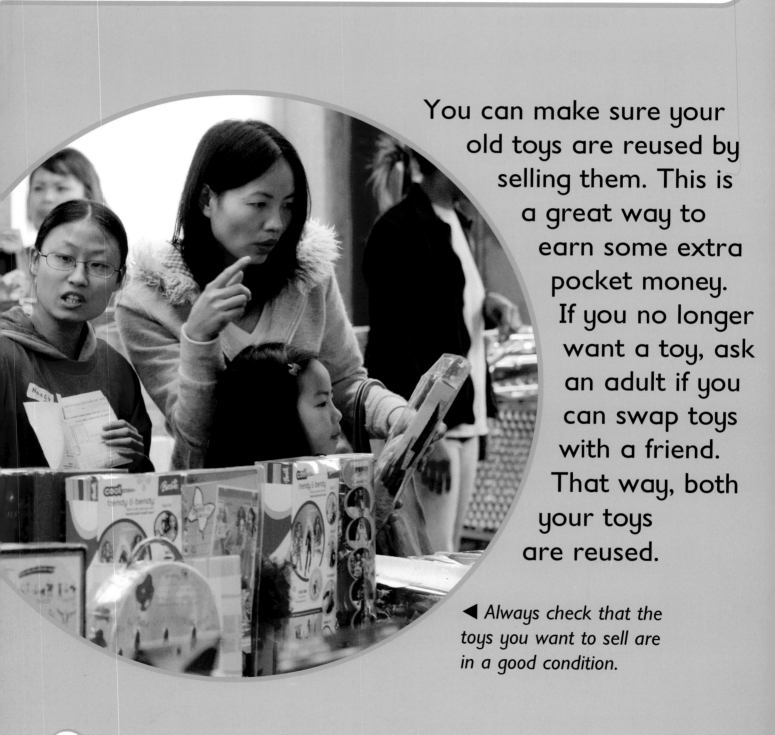

You can make sure your old toys are reused by selling them. This is a great way to earn some extra pocket money. If you no longer want a toy, ask an adult if you can swap toys with a friend. That way, both your toys are reused.

◄ *Always check that the toys you want to sell are in a good condition.*

Ask your teacher if you can start up a toy-swapping club at school. Another way to reuse toys is to join a toy library. Toy libraries are just like ordinary libraries, except you borrow toys, not books. You can also stay in the library to play with the toys, too.

▼ Toy libraries are good places to borrow all kinds of toys.

Toy recycling

If you break a toy, ask an adult to repair it for you. If it can't be repaired, maybe it can be recycled. Look at the material your old toy is made of. Wood and some kinds of metal can be recycled, so take toys made from these materials to a recycling center.

▼ *This woman is sorting through books and toys to see which ones can be recycled.*

You can make new toys from recycled materials, for example, you can cut up an old fleece or furry jacket to make a soft toy. You can also make accessories for your toys out of toy packaging, for example, you could use a box to make a home for one of your favorite toys.

▲ These cars are made from aluminum cans.

TRY SOME JUNK-MODELING

1. Make a rag doll from old scraps of material.

2. Use an odd sock to make a sock puppet.

3. Make a pom-pom from some old yarn.

4. Cut up some plastic bags to make a kite, using thin wooden dowels to make the frame.

Make a multicolored coat

Secondhand clothes can be made into something new, for example, it is easy to make a coat from an old shirt. You could sew some more material onto the bottom of the shirt to make it longer. Ask an adult to help you do this.

YOU WILL NEED:

1. a large, old shirt,
2. some scraps of bright-colored material,
3. paper, pencils, and felt-tip pens,
4. safety scissors,
5. pins,
6. craft glue.

1. Start making your coat by cutting the collar and cuffs off the shirt.

2. Draw the outline of your coat on some paper, showing it from the front and the back. Design a simple pattern for your coat, and color it in.

3. Enlarge your design on a photocopier to make copies of the patterns.

4. Cut out the paper patterns and pin them onto your scraps of colored material. Then cut out the shapes and glue them to your coat.

5. Wait for all the glue to dry before you try your coat on.

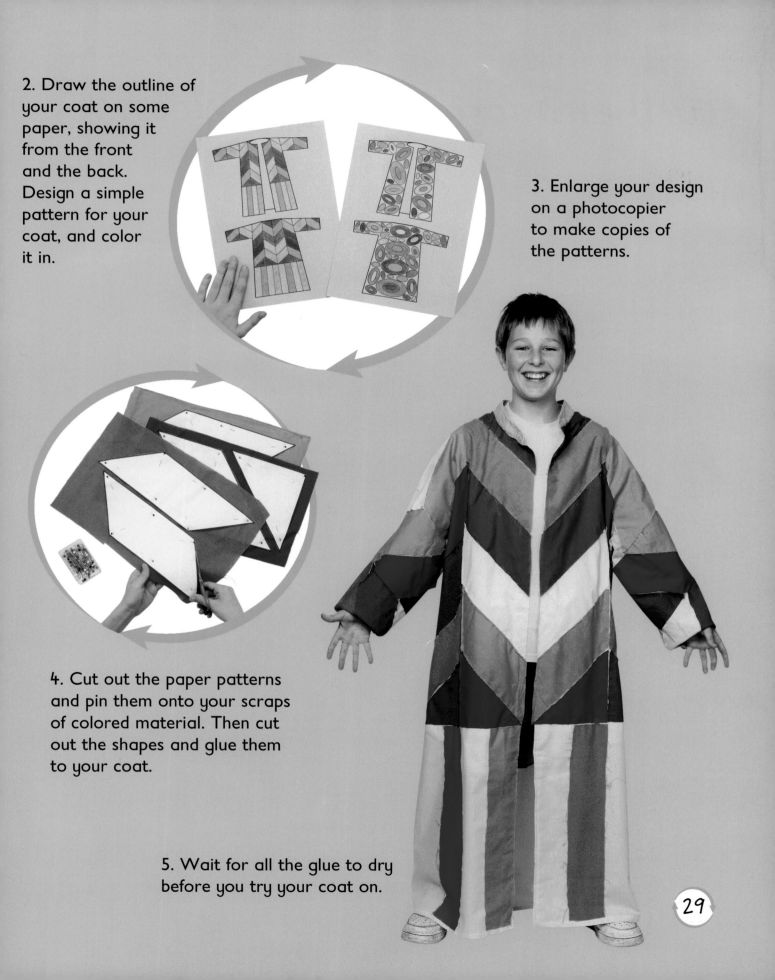

Further Information and Web Sites

Topic map

SCIENCE

Dig two holes in the yard. Bury a wooden craft stick in one hole, and a plastic straw in the other. After three months, dig up the stick and the straw. You'll see that wood rots quickly but plastic doesn't.

MATH

Hold a toy sale and invite your friends. Put price tags on all the toys, and make sure you give the right change for them. Add up all the money you make at the sale.

ENGLISH

Write a story about a toy that is saved from the trash can and sold at a thrift store. Give your story a sad beginning, and a happy ending!

GEOGRAPHY

Find out about a recent natural disaster, such as a flood or an earthquake. Where did it happen? Did any charities send food and clothes to help the people who were affected?

ART

Customize a pair of jeans and a T-shirt from a thrift store. Ask an adult to help you use fabric paint, and glue on patches to create your own style.

CLUB

Start a toy-swapping club at school. Encourage your friends to share and reuse toys, rather than buying new ones.

Further reading

Environment Action: Recycle by Kay Barnham (Crabtree Publishing, 2007)
Recycling and Re-using Clothes by Ruth Thomson (Smart Apple Media, 2006)
Reducing and Recycling Waste by Carol Inskipp (Gareth Stevens Publishing, 2005)

Web Sites

Due to the changing nature of Internet links, PowerKids Press has developed an online list of Web sites related to the subject of this book. This site is updated regularly. Please use this link to access this list:
http://www.powerkidslinks.com/reduce/clothes/

Glossary

bleached	to have color removed	**online**	using the Internet
chemical	a substance, or mixture of different substances	**pollution**	dirt in the air, water, or earth
clothing bank	a place where you can leave clothes to be recycled	**population**	the people who live in a place
		raw material	natural materials
condition	the state of something	**rechargeable**	a source of energy that can be reused
decay	to rot or spoil		
donate	giving items away to charity	**recycle**	when something is made into a new product
dyed	adding color to a material	**recycling bank**	a place where you can leave items to be recycled
electricity	a kind of energy used to make things work		
energy	the power to work	**recycling center**	a center where waste materials are recycled
environment	the world around us, and all living things		
fuel	something that is burned to make power	**reduce**	to cut back or make smaller
furnace	a hot oven in which things are burned	**reuse**	when something is used again
incinerator	a very hot furnace in which garbage is burned	**shoe bank**	where shoes can be dropped off to be reused or recycled
landfill site	a big garbage dump, where waste is buried underground	**textile**	a type of cloth made from threads or woven fabric
man-made	something made that is not found naturally	**thrift store**	a store that sells secondhand things to raise money
material	cloth or fabric		
natural	something found naturally	**unraveled**	undo something that is knitted together
natural disaster	an event of nature, e.g. a hurricane		

Index

Numbers in **bold** refer to a photograph.